Contents

There's no need for humans to create the dream pet of the twenty-first century...it is known as the Budgerigar, "Budgie" for short.

INTRODUCING THE BUDGERIGAR

In the future scientists may be able to design pets to order. They'll probably start by making up a list of qualities the dream pet should possess: beauty, intelligence, gentleness, hardiness, love for its owner, and the ability to thrive in small apartments on low-cost diets. It would also be nice if the pet were inexpensive and came in a range of decorator colors. And wouldn't it be terrific if it could whistle a pretty

The Budgerigar possesses a long list of good qualities. It is beautiful, intelligent, gentle, hardy, affectionate...not to mention inexpensive to keep.

tune or even talk?

There's no need for humans to create the dream pet of the twenty-first century. Nature, in the semiarid Australian interior, shaped this friendly, sociable, and hardy pet millenia ago. Scientists named it *Melopsittacus undulatus*. We call it the Budgerigar, "Budgie" for short.

We may also call it one of several other names, although we're usually creating some confusion in the process. Most people in the United States habitually refer to the Budgerigar as the "parakeet," an imprecise name because many other species of parrots are also called parakeets. At least many of these other parakeets resemble the Budgerigar in making good pets and fine talkers, and no real harm is done if the readers of certain historical novels get the mistaken impression that Alexander the Great was charmed by a snub-beaked Budgie! A more dangerous nickname for the Budgie was "lovebird." This title was encouraged in the 1920s when a Japanese prince bought a then rare blue pair for his fiancée, sparking a Japanese fashion for giving Budgies as a token of love. Since the true lovebird has a very different personality from the Budgerigar, a confused pet buyer could be in for a real disappointment; fortunately, this mistaken usage has just about vanished. Other names that you may or may not encounter include shell parakeet, warbling parakeet, or canary parrot.

Incidentally, the Budgie's full common name comes from the one quality not important in the dream pet—its taste! The word "Budgerigar" derives from an Australian Aboriginal term that means "good food."

ITS LIFE IN THE WILD

The wild Budgie is a social bird, traveling in flocks containing up to one hundred birds. These flocks often gather into clouds of hundreds of thousands or even millions of individuals. Since the rainfall in the Australian interior is irregular and unpredictable, Budgies are strong fliers that follow food and water rather than migrating according to some fixed pattern. When they chance upon a good supply of both, they waste no time going to nest to produce as many young as they possibly can before the opportunity passes. Tough and adaptable, they triumph over their harsh environment, replacing their population quickly even after such disasters as the drought of 1932, and the widespread brush fires of 1974, both of which took the lives of millions of Budgerigars.

It's this challenging environment that makes the Budgie the pet it is. Adapted to foraging in arid and semiarid grasslands rather than lush tropical rainforests, it survives and even reproduces on simple seed diets that would kill many other parrot species. Born to travel and breed in constant contact with its own kind, it is gentle and easy-going, qualities that make it an ideal companion for small children as well as a cheerful and cooperative flock member. Forced to actively hunt for the best breeding conditions rather than passively follow a fixed migration route, it's alert, intelligent, and eager to communicate—qualities that make for a wonderful and trainable pet.

To test the Budgerigar's hardiness scientists denied water to ten laboratory specimens. At 80°F and 30% humidity, the birds did well and lost little weight, even after 38 days without drinking. At lower temperatures, some individuals survived for over 4 months without water. It's worth noting that the Australian environment produced two other popular, hardy pet birds, the Zebra Finch and the Cockatiel.

The wild Budgie is similar to the Normal Light Green bird seen in captivity, although the wild bird tends to be quite a bit smaller. With its golden head and striped back, it resembles a sun-dappled leaf when it sits quietly on its favorite perch in a eucalyptus tree. An entire flock of ten to one hundred birds sharing the same tree, are amazingly hard to spot. Their ability to sit

The Budgerigar is alert, intelligent, and eager to communicate— qualities that make for a wonderful and trainable pet.

incredibly still (a technique that helps their bodies conserve water) also aids their disguise as a tree full of bright flowers and young leaves. The few differently colored wild Budgies usually don't survive because they're so easily picked out by predators.

The eucalyptus provides nesting holes as well as protective coloration, and whenever possible, the whole flock will try to nest in one tree, even if some pairs must make their homes in the tangle of roots on the ground. If food and water permit, the race against time to produce young begins as if at the sound of a shot. Any pairs not yet in breeding condition are soon stimulated by the sight of the busy pairs around them. The cock and hen quickly form an efficient partnership that yields healthy young in a short time. The hen incubates the eggs without interruption, the male bringing food to the female so that she doesn't have to leave the nest. When the young are first hatched, the cock continues to feed his hen, while she in turn gives the hatchlings predigested food regurgitated from her crop. When the chicks are a little larger, she leaves the nesthole to help her mate find food for the demanding babies. Still later, if conditions permit, she'll start laying the next clutch while the male weans the fledglings. The quick, efficient breeding habits of the Budgerigar are another reason, of course, that these lively birds have become affordable common pets.

VARIETIES

Today, you can walk into the smallest pet store and examine Budgies in a range of colors. Once human

Today, we can walk into the smallest pet store and examine Budgies in a wide range of colors.

project by buying the dark grays that would be produced along the way. It may not be possible to develop a red Budgie, since it's a primary color that can't be created by mixing the pigments already present in the Budgie's genes. But you never know. Blue is also a primary color, and it's easily produced in these birds, thanks to an optical quirk that couldn't have been predicted ahead of time. Perhaps one day a lucky breeder will find that some unexpected combination of birds has produced the long-awaited red Budgie. Some eager breeders have tried to help the process along by mating Budgies with some of the small grass parakeets that do possess a red pigment, but so far all of these hybrids have proved sterile.

Don't be fooled by sellers offering Budgies that have been fed color food or even dyed to produce a temporarily pink or reddish bird. The breeder who succeeds in producing the red Budgie won't have to look for buyers! In 1927, a pair of the new blue Budgies went for as much as $1,000. Taking into account the much greater difficulty in encountering and developing a red Budgie, not to mention the effects of the intervening years of high inflation, a red Budgie breeder could certainly command a much, much higher price.

But you needn't spend a king's ransom to get a perfect pet in a beautiful color. Lovely blue, white, yellow, and green Budgies are all available at roughly the same price. Since color and pattern have no effect on the Budgie's personality, you can get the prettiest bird in the shop without sacrificing a thing in terms of friendliness, gentleness, or intelligence. No need to worry about that beautiful Sky Blue Budgie turning out to have a fussy, fancy personality; the pretty Budgie is just as sweet as a plain one. Take your time, have fun looking them over, and feel free to go for the one you want.

You needn't spend a king's ransom to get a perfect pet in a beautiful color. Lovely blue, white, yellow, and green budgies are all available at roughly the same price.

CHOOSING YOUR BUDGERIGAR

Almost every home or lifestyle has room for Budgies, but not everyone has room for one Budgie. Contradictory? Not at all. Remember, the Budgerigar is an extremely social bird. It may live longer without water than without companionship! In the early days of Budgie keeping, many people believed that these birds would die if kept from their mates. They were only partially correct. Sex and courtship are hard work for these conscientious birds, and unmated Budgies actually have a longer life expectancy than good breeders. It's lack of love and companionship that's fatal. If you don't have the time to spend with your Budgie virtually every day, it will become depressed and susceptible to disease, sometimes even mutilating itself by tearing out its own feathers. If you travel or party frequently, or spend long hours at the office, you shouldn't try to keep a single pet Budgie. Get two and let these cheerful little socialites entertain each other.

Conversely, if you are a parent selecting a child's pet, or an invalid or a home office worker who requires a companion to share long hours each day, you should opt for a single Budgie. Don't get a pair, hoping to train both birds at once; they'll be too involved with playing with one another to

get interested in their lessons.

CHOOSING A HEALTHY BUDGIE

No matter what the time of year, you won't have much trouble finding Budgies for sale. Bred indoors, with abundant food and water,

Your local pet shop will have a wide selection of books by T.F.H. for you to read up on the care and maintenance of Budgies.

they can and do breed in any season. Many excellent birds are available in spring, since breeders of exhibition Budgies start their pairs in late winter or early spring in order to allow plenty of time to prepare for the autumn shows. After

selecting the young nearest the "ideal," these breeders sell the others to stores or individuals. These culls may not be as beefy or come in as many rare colors as the top show quality birds, but they can make wonderfully entertaining and attractive pets. Christmastime also finds plenty of lovable Budgies for sale, especially inexpensive specimens bred in aviaries specifically for the pet trade.

Whether you buy your Budgie from a shop, an aviary, or the back room of somebody's home, you need to look for evidence of health and care. Cleanliness is essential. Although any place where many birds are bred may become somewhat dusty, the dust situation shouldn't be raging so far out of control that you can't breathe without violent sneezing. Certainly, there shouldn't be any offensive odors! Budgies are naturally tidy individuals. As seed-eaters, they produce compact, odorless feces that fall neatly to the bottom of the cage; as strong fliers, they spend a great deal of time keeping their feathers clean and ready for use. If their cages and plumage are filthy, you can bet that they've either come down with an illness or are just about to.

The primary hallmark of a good seller is concern. That means concern for the birds, who won't be so crowded together that they've started fighting and yanking out one another's feathers, as well as concern for you. A concerned seller will ask if you have a proper cage—an individual breeder might not have them for sale anyway—but to make sure the Budgie will have a safe home. The seller should also be willing to answer any questions you may have about bird care in general or the proposed pet in particular.

Before you buy, examine the Budgie as closely as possible to confirm that it's in good health. You may feel sorry for a saggy, moth-eaten bird, but you shouldn't take it into your home. Besides the obvious chance of losing the animal and infecting any other birds you may own, you're imposing an additional stress at a time when the Budgie isn't fit enough to cope. It must remain the seller's responsibility to cure a sick bird before trying to market it. Yes, it's quite possible that the only thing wrong with the bird is that it's being bullied because it's at the bottom of the pecking order in an overcrowded cage. But how can you know for sure that this stress hasn't already weakened the bird enough to let in some serious infection? The best way you can help such animals is by taking your money to another seller, so that stores and breeders will have an economic incentive to stop crowding birds.

Apart from obvious feather damage, discharge from the eyes, nose, and vent are all serious symptoms, as are feces caked thickly around the vent. A deformed beak or weak, twisted legs can indicate an inherited defect or the incurable legacy of an early nutritional problem. Although the bird may sit very still, as if hoping to avoid drawing your attention, it should certainly be alert and responsive when you come near. If all else checks out, ask the seller to catch the Budgie for your inspection. Probe under its feathers gently. If the keelbone (located in the chest) feels like the blade of a knife, the bird is too underweight to endure the stress of relocation. If you feel strange bumps or swelling, the bird may be one of the many Budgerigars plagued by harmful tumors and must be rejected.

Some Budgies have an odd ring of feathers on their heads. That isn't a problem, it's a crest! Three kinds of crests exist: the tufted, which consists of just a few raised feathers on top of the head, the half-crested, which has a small neat cap, and the full-crested, which seems to have an early Beatles' style hairdo. Since they're hard to breed reliably and may have health problems, crested Budgies are usually not offered to beginners. If you do get a crested Budgie, remember never to pair it with another crested, since the offspring of such unions has a very low survival rate.

Before you buy, examine the Budgie as closely as possible to confirm that it's in good health.

CHOOSING THE BEST PET

If you want a true feathered companion, a bird that will play with you, spend

hours riding around the house on your shoulder, and even learn to do tricks and talk, choose a Budgie that's young and adaptable. It isn't necessary to buy a handfed baby (although that's certainly nice if one is available) since Budgies are easily trained up to the age of 3 months. The younger, the better, of course, as long as the babies are weaned and able to feed themselves, a process that should be finished by 6 weeks.

It's easy to make sure that a Budgie is young enough to make a good pet for a beginner. Babies' heads and necks are covered with a network of shell-like stripes that start to disappear at 10 or 12 weeks. Babies also look big-eyed because the iris (ring of color surrounding the pupil) is black; as they mature, this ring lightens noticeably. Very young babies have darker

If you want a true feathered companion, a bird that will play with you, spend hours riding around the house on your shoulder, and even learn to do tricks and talk, choose a Budgie that's young and adaptable.

beaks; if a prospective pet is feeding itself, yet still has some black on the beak, it's at the perfect age for training as a companion.

CHOOSING A PAIR

If you have little time to spend training your birds, but would like some color and life in your home, you will have to pick two healthy Budgies. Age isn't as crucial since you won't be training them as pets, but it does reduce stress on the birds if they are moved

into their new home while young, especially if they have come from an aviary where they weren't used to living in close contact with admiring humans every day. Feel free to mix and match colors as you please; Budgies have no prejudices!

Are you wondering how to get a "true" pair—one boy, one girl? Adult budgies are relatively easy to sex, at least when you compare them to some species of parrots that look so much alike it's a mystery how they themselves can tell. The general rule involves checking the cere, the flesh around the nostrils. In most males, at least while in breeding condition, the cere is bright blue, while most females have brown ceres. Some Budgies, however, particularly among the lighter color forms, may have ceres that look blue in one light, pinkish tan in another. What is it? Only Mother Nature knows for sure.

Don't worry. Unless you're a serious breeder, in which case you will begin to develop the sensitive eye necessary to sex Budgies correctly most of the time, you needn't be concerned. A pair of Budgies will enjoy playing with each other just as much if they turn out to be members of the same sex. They won't be able to breed, of course, but most single pairs don't breed in any case. Because they're colony breeders, they rarely get the urge to reproduce unless they see other Budgies around them doing the same thing. If you do want to try breeding, start with two or three pairs containing birds of known sex.

WELCOMING THE NEW BUDGIE

The first few days in its new home are important to the Budgie. Don't make it spend this crucial period of orientation in a cardboard box or an undersized travel cage! The permanent cage should be ready and waiting for the new pet in a quiet, draft-free location. A low-key corner of a den or living room is great because it allows the bird to observe the comings and goings of family members without feeling under observation itself. The kitchen, on the other hand, must be off-limits because of cooking odors, aerosol sprays, and other respiratory irritants that can overwhelm a small bird's system. Be especially careful to keep the Budgie away from freshly painted rooms or natural gas.

If the new pet isn't yet tame, it will be understandably cautious about its new environment. Don't rush it. Let it spend the first few days looking around and getting acquainted with the surroundings. In addition to its usual seed cup and water bowl, scatter some small seed or a strand of millet spray along the floor in case the nervous Budgie reverts to its ground-feeding instincts. Keep an eye on the Budgie, but don't pester it with attention for the moment. Give it time to relax enough to eat and drink before you consider taming.

Budgies can sit very still, especially if they don't want to be noticed, so don't be alarmed if your new pet is sitting there like a little stone. It will come around. You just need to give it a chance to figure out that no one is going to hurt it. The young Budgie will probably start eating sooner if you start it on the same food it was fed by the seller. Any changes in diet should be reserved for a

less stressful period. Don't expect to see the Budgie eat; it probably won't crack seed in front of you until it trusts you better. In the unusual event that you don't find empty seed husks on the bottom of the cage or within its bowl after 24 hours, you may then conclude that the bird isn't eating and contact the seller for help.

Most likely, your Budgie will be eating by the next day, resigned to its new home if not yet delighted with it. At this point, you'll be ready to tame and train your new pet, helping it become a member of the family as well as a beloved avian companion.

Do not make your new Budgie spend its first few days in its new home in a cardboard box or an undersized travel cage! The permanent cage should be ready and waiting for the new pet in a quiet, draft-free location.

YOUR BUDGERIGAR'S HOME

If you've never kept a pet bird before, you may have the idea that a tame Budgie doesn't really need a cage. Some people even feel that they're doing their bird a kindness by letting it have the freedom of the house at all hours of the day and night. Wrong! Like most pet birds, the Budgie likes having a place of its own where it can retreat to eat and drink, sleep unmolested, or just rest up until it's ready for the next round of family play. Unless its cage is cruelly confining or it's trapped there for days on end without attention, the Budgie considers the cage its home.

Although you certainly should allow your Budgie plenty of free flight time when you're home to supervise, you also need a cage to keep the Budgie safe while you're out of the house. Otherwise, your curious winged pet could easily stumble onto some fatal mischief. If you have children, you know how difficult it is to childproof the average home against a crawling, relatively weak toddler. Multiply the difficulties involved when it's a sturdy little hookbill who can fly up to seek out trouble if it can't find any on the ground, and you start to get an idea of the magnitude of the problem. Furthermore, the tiny Budgie can poison itself on a bit of houseplant or a dab of spilled chemical that the much larger child wouldn't

even notice. Even if you're a scrupulous housekeeper, you can't hope to see your Budgie live out a normal lifespan if you allow it to roam free in your absence.

Therefore, you need a cage. But what kind of cage? Don't expect it to live in one of those small traveling cages sometimes included in package deals. Unless someone is with the bird all day so that it only has to return to the cage to eat and sleep, that tiny area simply isn't enough for an active,

with a pet parrot all day? When you can't be with your Budgie, it will be in its cage and it will both want and need room enough to turn around without crimping its tail!

lively bird. Please be realistic before nodding your head and saying, "Yeah, yeah, I'm home all the time. He can sleep in the traveler." You may be home, but will your shoulder really be available at all hours to serve as the Budgie's playpen? Are there really never days when you feel too harassed or busy or just plain sick to keep up

Because the cage will be a play area as well as a bedroom, I strongly advise that you choose one at least 2 feet in length for a single pet Budgie. A pair also needs a minimum of 2' x $1\frac{1}{2}$' x $1\frac{1}{2}$'. Don't scrimp. Yes, the pet shop probably did keep several Budgies in the same amount of an area space because these birds are good-natured enough to tolerate somewhat crowded accommodations temporarily. But no one intends you to believe that the birds could live like that permanently! When deciding between two cages, let space, not price, be your guide. Even a tiny Budgie likes to spread its wings and get comfortable when it's at home.

The ideal Budgie cage will have horizontal bars running less than a $1/2$ inch apart to let the bird scramble about for exercise. If the bars are too far apart, there is the chance that the Budgie will accidentally choke itself by forcing its curious head between them.

Although not the powerful chewers most parrots are, Budgies do require metal cages. By concentrating their patient beaks on a favorite spot, the Budgie will soon work an ugly hole into a wooden or bamboo cage. (I'd give the average Budgie about two weeks to reduce the latter to a pile of matchsticks!) If you buy a painted cage, get it from a reputable pet shop or pet supply house. Secondhand cages spruced up for a garage sale share a common problem with ritzy department store decorator models: lead. Unless the cage was prepared by someone who knows birds, it may have a poisonous lead-based paint job or lead solder connection that could kill a chewing bird. Many antique or decorator cages are also way too small to make humane homes for a Canary, much less an active Budgie.

After size and safety, you may consider your own convenience. Both you and your Budgie will prefer a cage that's easy to clean. If it's painted, the color should be baked on to prevent the casual chipping that provides places for bacteria or molds to hide. In any case, a removable tray bottom is essential to easy removal of the wastes that fall to the bottom of the cage. A shallow tray must be lined with paper (which must be changed every day) or else rinsed off daily, while a deeper tray may be filled with a corncob or pine shavings litter that can be changed every two or three days. Whichever seems easiest to you is fine.

I should also mention that it's wise to choose a cage with a door that can be locked open as well as closed. When you're at home, you'll often want the door open so that your pet can exit at will. Otherwise, you may find yourself running back and forth to the cage to find out whether the Budgie's ready to play, or worse, you'll forget about the poor thing entirely.

Strictly speaking, a cage cover isn't a necessity for a pet bird, but I really find it invaluable. You don't need to worry about drafts if you've been careful to place the Budgie in a draft-free spot, but a cage cover is far more than a fabric windbreak! Placed on the cage at the same time each evening, it informs the Budgie that it's time to rest and shuts out distracting noises and lights.

Your local pet store will stock a variety of decorative cages that will suit the needs of your new pet Budgie. Photo courtesy of Penn Plax.

If the bars of your Budgie's cage are too far apart, there is the chance that the Budgie will accidentally choke itself by forcing its curious head between them.

Perhaps even more important, it tells visitors that the Budgie is resting and discourages all but the most hopeless from annoying a bird that's ready for sleep.

Where to put the cage? As I mentioned earlier, any place where the Budgie can easily interact with the family without being subjected to constant noisy traffic. Higher is better because birds feel more secure when they can look down on others, but I don't particularly care for hanging the cage from a hook, especially in a "swingy" position. Any sturdy shelf or stand is nice, but please don't expect the Budgie to sleep atop the TV or a stereo

speaker. (Birds usually learn to like the music you like, but not if they can hear it reverberating through their hollow bones!) Remember to avoid drafts, natural gas or other sources of strong odor, and direct sun. No, you can't place that Budgie in a window! Even desert birds can

You must be careful what type of birds you pair your pet Budgie with. It is best to only house it with another Budgie.

move into the shade if it gets too hot. Penned in an overheated, sunny area, the usually sturdy Budgie can suffer a fatal heatstroke.

PERCHES AND TOYS

If your Budgie cage comes with plastic perches, replace them immediately. Wooden perches are far better for your pet's feet and toes. For comfort's sake, choose a perch wide enough to allow the Budgie to wrap its toes about three-quarters of the

way around. Place them strategically so that a sitting Budgie won't defecate into its food and water dishes; if you can't manage this, the cage is too small. Scrape the perches once a week with a perch scraper from the pet shop or some good sandpaper to prevent the buildup of feces. Don't expect perches to last forever, though. A good perch is temporary because it tempts the beak as well as the foot, keeping both bill and toenails trim.

If you have a choice between round, oval, and square perches, pick one of each. The Budgie's feet will be less problem-prone if the bird doesn't have to sit exactly the same way all the time. An excellent way to exercise feet, toes, and beak is to provide a natural branch for perching and chewing. Fruit tree, willow,

Budgies are good-enough to tolerate somewhat crowded accommodations TEMPORARILY.

shower, but you should also discourage it from bathing under a dripping tap since it could be scalded if those droplets are hot. Otherwise, relax and enjoy the pleasure

Budgies regularly groom themselves, however, there are certain matters in which they require the help of their owner. A good nutritional diet and attention paid to claws are essential on the owner's part.

that only a desert animal can display when it encounters fresh cool water.

GOOD GROOMING

A domesticated parrot rarely gets enough claw exercise to keep its toenails sufficiently worn down, and Budgies are no exception. It isn't hard to clip a tame Budgie's toenails, but you may want to visit a pet grooming shop or a vet to see how it's done before you

try it yourself. Special bird nail clippers are available, but I find that a small pair of dog nail clippers work just as well. You should also have some styptic powder or a bit of flour on hand in case you accidentally nip into the vein and must staunch the subsequent bleeding.

Experts can clip a tame Budgie themselves, but a beginner should enlist the aid of a partner. Have your helper hold the Budgie in a dry towel, with the towel draped loosely over its head so that it won't see the clippers. The affable Budgie may not care for being held like this, but it will probably resign itself to chewing on the towel. If you hold up its foot to a good light, you will see where the vein runs through the nail. Clip a small portion from the end, carefully avoiding the vein. It's better to take too little nail than too much; you can always repeat a tentative job in a week, but you may be too rattled to clip ever again if you've made your pet bleed. Stay calm if you do hit the vein, a bit of

Above: Beginners are not advised to attempt to trim a Budgie's beak. Consult your vet or see a pet groomer for help if your bird's beak seems misshapen or deformed.

Below: Clipping a few feathers to prevent your pet Budgie from sailing out the door is a good idea.

Above: A professional will know the proper way to hold your pet Budgie to clip its beak, nails, or wings.

Below: You may want to watch someone else clip your pet's wings before you try it. When you are ready to do it yourself...extend one wing and clip several of the primary feathers.

flour or styptic powder will quickly stop the bleeding, and your miffed Budgie will feel more forgiving when it realizes it can perch comfortably again.

I don't advise that beginners attempt to trim a Budgie's beak. Consult your vet or see a pet groomer for help if your bird's beak seems misshapen or deformed. You can prevent many problems in this area by providing plenty of chewtoys for the Budgie to demolish.

What about wing-clipping? Although few people would argue with the need to keep the wings of larger parrots clipped, there is quite a controversy over the clipping of a Budgie's wings. The large parrots, after all, exercise largely through climbing rather than flying, so that little mobility is lost when their wings are clipped

for reasons of safety. Budgies, however, are naturally strong fliers who can become quite obese if they cannot fly.

Aviary or paired Budgies who rarely leave their cages probably shouldn't have their wings clipped. On the other hand, a pet Budgie who spends a great deal of time out of its cage probably should. Clipping a few feathers to prevent it from sailing out the door or into the ceiling fan is a good compromise since it can still "hop" short distances about the house for exercise and companionship. Squeamishness about pain isn't a consideration; unlike the operation called pinioning (commonly performed on waterfowl) in which a bone is removed from the wing, wing-clipping is as painless as trimming hair.

Again, you may want to watch someone else clip your pet's wings before you try it. When you are ready to do it yourself, employ your helper to hold the Budgie in the towel while you extend one wing and clip several of the primary feathers (found in what would be the elbow to wrist area in a human arm). Don't clip too close to the bird's body or you may encounter "blood feathers." Since these feathers are still growing, you would draw blood if you accidentally cut them.

FEEDING THE BUDGERIGAR

The Budgie is often called a vegetarian, and many people interpret that description to mean their pet needs nothing but seed and water. While it's true many hardy Budgies scrape by on this marginal diet, you must be aware that it isn't enough to protect your bird's health indefinitely. Since Budgies are so easy to feed, there's no reason not to do it right. A quick overview of Budgie nutrition will give you a better understanding of what your pet requires to live out its lifespan of some 12 to 16 years.

All animals require six basic elements: protein, carbohydrate, fat, vitamins, minerals, and water. The Budgie, as we've seen, can struggle by without water for quite a while, but when we keep a bird in captivity it's only fair to have a water source available to it at all times since we can't read its mind and know precisely when it does wish to drink. In fact, for the sake of cleanliness, we should change open cups of water daily, just as we would with any other bird. However, since Budgies do drink at irregular intervals, I tend to feel less concern about possible impurities present in tap water, although I still think it's advisable to remove traces of chlorine by serving cooled boiled water. If you have other kinds of birds, as I do, you'll soon find it just as easy to offer the Budgie pure

spring or distilled water along with all the others. I don't fret about the minute quantities of minerals the Budgie misses when it drinks distilled rather than spring or tap water for two reasons; there are other easy ways to provide minerals and the Budgie doesn't drink enough water for me to rely on it as a decent mineral source anyway. For similar reasons, I suspect that adding

vitamin and mineral supplements to a Budgie's water is pretty much a waste of time and money.

THE BASICS OF BUDGIE NUTRITION

Before we can formulate a good Budgie diet, we need to know what these birds eat in the wild. Fortunately, the beloved Budgie has been closely studied in its native

habitat to provide us with this valuable information. As it forages over the ground, the Budgie consumes various seed grasses in all stages of ripeness, along with the occasional insect. Because they range far and wide, ingesting many varieties of vegetable and animal matter, Budgies in the wild meet their nutritional needs without planning. Since we don't have

Since Budgies are so easy to feed, there's no reason not to do it correctly.

the same variety of seeds (much less insects!) in our stores and homes, we have to choose a little more carefully for our trusting pet.

The first element of concern is protein, the building block

of animal life. Without protein, a bird cannot grow, replace lost feathers, heal injuries, fight infection, or reproduce. To help the young Budgies grow up quickly, the parent birds feed the nestlings a mixture of regurgitated food and a substance called "crop milk," a high protein baby food formed from the cell walls of the parent's crop. Without sufficient protein, the parents are physically exhausted and unable to feed their young enough to grow properly. Since protein is also required in egg formation, female Budgies are at special risk from low protein diets. Infection and even death can result.

At first, the wild Budgie diet seem suspiciously low in

Your pet Budgie should be offered a variety of seed mixtures. Many varieties of seed mixtures are available from your local pet shop to provide your pet with all the necessary dietary requirements.

protein. Although insects (like all animal bodies) are good sources of this nutrient, seeding grasses are considered poor sources because they're "incomplete." That means that a particular kind of seed tends to be low in one or another of the amino acids that make up a complete protein. Since the body can't use a substance as a protein unless *all* of the amino acids are present, it might appear that the Budgie's wild diet is dangerously deficient. But by sampling many different kinds of seeding grasses, the wild Budgie can make up the amino acid deficit that would appear if it consumed only one or two kinds of grasses. Of course, at home, where we don't have access to unlimited types of seed, we do well to supplement the pet Budgie's diet with known sources of complete protein.

Furthermore, it has been shown that domesticated Budgies have a higher protein requirement than wild ones, at least when growing and

Budgies require feeding dishes that are easily accessible and that hold a good quantity of seed. Photo courtesy of Penn Plax.

breeding. Because they're substantially larger than the wild specimens yet must mature in the same amount of time, baby domesticated Budgies demand additional protein to sustain healthy growth. Show-quality Budgies, intentionally bred for impressive size, have an especially high need for protein during the crucial nestling and fledgling stages.

Fortunately, excellent complete proteins are readily available for Budgies. The new pelleted feeds scientifically formulated to meet protein and nutritional needs really can't be beat for convenience. Although expensive for breeders of many birds, especially for people who hope to see a profit, these feeds are quite reasonable for the pet owner or small hobby breeder. (If you don't believe me, figure out how much it would cost you to feed your cat or dog for the same period!) For those on a budget, the local poultry feed store has some excellent bargains on high-protein crumbles such as turkey or game bird starter. A time-honored taste-tempting protein is the hard boiled egg, well-mashed with a teaspoon of a good powdered avian vitamin/mineral supplement and human protein powder from the health food store. Although you should be careful to never leave egg mix out longer

Above: In the wild, the Budgie consumes various seed grasses in all stages of ripeness, along with the occasional insect.

Below: Spray millet is very much enjoyed by many birds. It is a special treat that should be fed only in addition to your Budgie's basic diet. This and other very nutritious "treats" are available at your local pet store.

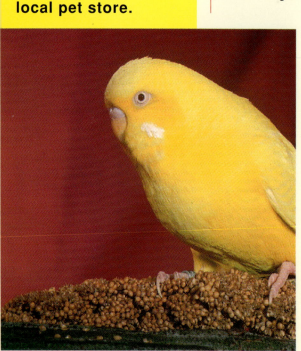

than 24 hours, you should remember this recipe for the Budgie who ignores other sources of protein.

Two other important elements in the Budgie diet are carbohydrate, the source of quick, easily digested energy, and fat, the source of steady, slow-burning energy as well as a compact substance for storing food in the body. Fat is also required to keep the feathers in condition. There is little problem getting enough of these substances in the diet unless an animal is starving, but if for some reason neither was available, the body could break down protein for an emergency energy source. (However,

neither carbohydrate nor fat can be reformed into protein, no matter how badly it's needed.) The basic seed diet is an excellent source of carbohydrate, while fats are an important component of the seeds found in commercial "tonic mixes." To prevent obesity, give a small amount of the tonic mix in a separate

Greens of all types are greatly appreciated by Budgies. The best greens are those which are darker in color because these have a high nutritional content.

treat cup no more than two or three times a week.

Vitamins are sadly lacking in cage-bird diets. The pelleted and other high protein foods are also sources of many vitamins, but old seed is frequently much lower in vitamins than you'd expect. If you have just one or two

An over indulged Budgie may quickly become overweight. In that case, restrict table foods to vegetables and fruits without dollops of dressing, butter, or margarine.

TAMING AND TRAINING

The younger the Budgie, the more success you'll have with training. A newly weaned youngster is ideal, while an adult can be close to untamable. Assuming you chose a youngster for your pet, however, you'll find the taming process easy and enjoyable even if you've never tamed a parrot before.

Whether or not you intend to keep the Budgie's wings clipped after it's tame, you should probably start by having the seller clip a few of the flight feathers. A Budgie raised by its own parents is naturally very shy of large humans, and you could traumatize it badly if you must chase it around the training room with a net! Also, it's safer if the bird gets to know the layout of the home before it's capable of an all-out flight into a win-

dow or wall. Do ask the seller to perform this chore since you don't want your pet to form its first impressions of you while you're holding it down to trim its feathers.

It's possible to hand-tame a young Budgie in fifteen minutes, although most people prefer to spread the

A baby Budgie is unlikely to bite you, especially if you take the gradual approach, and in any case, it will certainly not inflict any real damage.

process out over a period of days. If for some reason you're taming an adult or a previously abused bird, you *must* proceed slowly, rebuilding the Budgie's trust over a period of weeks or even months. Intensive taming helps you to take advantage of the Budgie's peak learning period between five and ten

The Budgie learns most quickly when it has nothing to distract it from the attentions of its trainer.

weeks of age, but since this method is quite stressful, it should be reserved for healthy, well-fed specimens no more than nine or ten weeks old.

Either a simple hand-held perch or a T-shaped perch called a T-stick is advisable to help taming go more smoothly. I don't suggest wearing gloves unless you are extremely nervous or sensitive to pain. The baby Budgie is unlikely to bite you, especially if you take the gradual approach, and in any case, it will certainly not inflict any real damage. By using the gloves, you have only added another step to the taming, since the bird will have to be taught later that it's safe to sit on your bare hand.

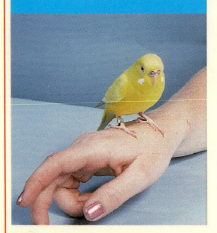

Your new pet Budgerigar will have to be taught that it is safe to sit on your bare hand.

INTENSIVE TAMING

Caution: This method should only be used for healthy, young Budgies who are eating well in their new home!

Although it's cracking seed, your new Budgie is probably most reluctant to leave its cage.

Open the cage. The Budgie is unlikely to leap for its freedom, as you may suppose; it usually prefers to cower behind bars. It's up to you to get it out.

It may not seem to do much at all, in fact, except sit very still and hope it's escaping notice. You may wonder if that quivering heap of feathers will really become a pet. Never fear! You should see it begin to gain its confidence this very night.

Clear the room containing the cage of all fragile knick knacks, spiny houseplants, drinking glasses, or other hazards. Cover any aquariums and windows. Close all doors, locking any that lead directly outside. Any pets must be moved to another room, and other birds should be out of earshot as well as out of sight. Turn off the TV and the stereo. The Budgie learns most quickly when it has nothing to distract it from the attentions of its

trainer. Only one person should handle the job of training, to avoid confusing the Budgie. It can be introduced to the rest of the family once it has had a chance to decide that humans are OK.

Now you may open the cage. The Budgie is unlikely to leap for its freedom, as you may suppose; it usually prefers to cower behind bars. It's up to you to get it out. Although you wouldn't put your hand in the cage of a large parrot, who even if tame would react with outrage to this invasion of its territory, it's perfectly safe to put your hand into your Budgie's cage. Slowly! Make

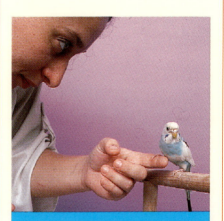

When you hold your finger at chest height— you may have to nudge the Budgie gently—it will eventually be unable to resist the temptation to step aboard.

your movements almost imperceptible, and talk in a low, soothing voice the whole time. If you can, approach the bird from its side so that it can see you clearly out of one eye. It will feel less threatened if you approach quietly, head-on

towards its blind spot, like a predator preparing to pounce!

The untame Budgie may flutter toward you as if to bite (but rarely doing more than feinting), or huddle away from you, crying with fear. Stop moving your hand forward when it panics, but don't retreat. Otherwise, it will think it can scare you off and repeat these behaviors whenever you attempt training. When it calms somewhat, slowly move your hand forward once more. Your aim is to sidle up to the Budgie's chest to take advantage of the bird's natural desire to step up. When you hold your finger at chest height—you may have to nudge the Budgie gently—it will eventually be unable to resist the temptation to step aboard. At that point, you may start to very slowly remove your hand from the cage. Be patient. The Budgie may hop off and on several times before you convince it to ride out into the open air. Notice the time. If more than fifteen or twenty minutes have

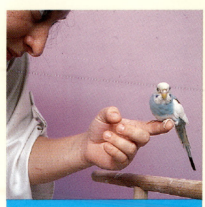

A bird that walks on you with confidence if not enthusiasm is technically tame, but it should be trained to be held in the hand.

passed, the session has gone on long enough. Praise the Budgie for stepping on your hand and let it step off onto its perch once more. You can return for the next session in an hour or two.

Once you've coaxed the Budgie into riding on your hand out into the room, it may become overwhelmed and try to fly away. It won't go far if its wings are clipped, so stand still repeating reassurances until it lands. Then fetch it by placing

your hand against its chest again. If it's in an awkward or high location, you can use the perch or T-stick to pick it up, but slowly transfer it to your hand when you can. After being fetched a few times, the Budgie will be tired and willing to sit still long enough to understand that it's safe. Again, if the session takes more than fifteen or twenty minutes, gently return it to the cage after it has successfully sat on your hand for a little while. If it's a fast learner, you can go directly to a game called "the ladder." With the Budgie resting on one finger, bring the other (always approaching from the side) to its chest. When it steps up, place the other finger at chest

height. Let the Budgie alternate between fingers until you're holding your arms over your head.

A bird that walks on you with confidence if not enthusiasm is technically tame, but I recommend a final taming step that will make your Budgie much easier to care for if it's ever sick or injured: teaching it to permit being held in the hand. It will probably never be thrilled about the treatment, but by its acceptance of bodily handling could literally make the difference between life and death if it must be examined by a vet. A Budgie can be picked up and held in one hand. Gently enclose the bird in your palm, holding the wings firmly to prevent injury but *never* pressing on the chest. Its head should remain free, with your thumb and index finger encircling the neck. The cries may be pitiful, but you will soon silence them if you take this opportunity to teach it about the joys of head-scratching. Approach slowly with your free hand and scratch gently about the area where its ears are hidden. The anguished complaints will shortly change to happy chirps, and a relaxed Budgie may even shut its eyes in bliss. Now you're on the way to getting a true pet!

GRADUAL TAMING

Most of you will probably prefer to take the gradual approach, and that's fine. For the first two weeks, you will slowly introduce yourself to the Budgie without removing it from the cage. Whenever you're near, talk to it in a soothing voice. Tell it its name and admire its appearance.

After two weeks of gradual taming, a young Budgie should be sitting confidently on your finger as you move it within the cage.

Move slowly and gracefully as you clean its tray and change its dishes, talking softly all the while. Periodically approach the cage with a small bit of greenfood or apple, offering it through the bars of the cage. Offer the treat at intervals throughout the day, but don't hover at the cage for more than ten minutes at a time. After a few days, you may start inserting your hand slowly into the cage as described in the previous section. If you are very fearful of biting or the bird seems unusually shy, you may find it easier to teach it to hop onto the perch before accepting the finger. Take your time, and don't try to do too much at once. Many short five-minute lessons throughout the day are better than a couple of half-hour sessions.

At the end of two weeks, a young Budgie should be sitting confidently on your finger as you move it within the cage. (Older birds will take longer.) At this point, you're ready to remove it from the cage into the room. Once it has gained confidence and is walking freely up your "ladder" or shoulder, you can move on to holding and head scratching. Never rush. You will probably want to spend several short sessions on each step to show your Budgie that it can trust you. By the age of three to four months, you can expect your Budgie to fly to you eagerly when it can. Many Budgies start showing affection even earlier.

THE WORD "NO"

If your Budgie tries to bite or has picked up something dangerous or inappropriate, you may wonder if you should punish it to make it learn to avoid hurting or being hurt. The answer is NO. Birds don't learn from punishment because they are too frightened. Remember how much bigger you are, and you will understand why a cuffed Budgie will be too busy fearing for its life to worry about what upset you. If you must stop the Budgie from doing something at once, you should say "No" in a loud voice as you remove it from the source of the problem. To stop biting, it's best to ignore the behavior. When the Budgie sees that biting doesn't work, it will drop the habit. (Don't be overly anxious about this possibility. A Budgie tamed early is un-likely to bite.) Sometimes beginners are nervous because they think a parrot is reaching down to bite when it's really just using its beak to steady itself. Again, if this worries you, start taming with a perch. You will soon see how gently the Budgie touches the perch with its beak when it's steadying itself.

TRICK TRAINING

Professional animal trainers, who train birds to do

You may find it easier to teach your pet Budgie to hop onto a perch before accepting your finger.

One of the most valuable tricks you can teach your Budgie is to "come" on command. Once it's flying freely to your shoulder, you should have little difficulty with this trick.

tricks by teaching them to associate certain actions with a food reward, can make successful performing artists of Budgies and other birds that are not even technically tame. However, at home trick training is usually based on affection. The Budgie shows off to win a beloved human's admiration, with a food treat being only a secondary enticement for a good performance. Therefore, a tame Budgie who loves its owner will learn tricks much faster than an untame bird.

One of the most valuable tricks you can teach your Budgie is to "come" on command. Once it's flying freely to your shoulder, you should have little difficulty with this trick. Place the Budgie on top of its playpen or cage, and tell it to "come." Have a food treat ready for when it obeys. Of course, the first few times it may fly to you simply because it wants to, it has no idea it's doing a trick at all. But if you practice faithfully, rewarding the Budgie each time it comes to you on command, it should eventually learn to associate the word with the desired action. A sharp Budgie may even learn to say the word "come" itself, and to be fair, I guess you better obey!

Very patient people have also taught their Budgies to defecate on command in their playpens or cages. It's easier just to wear a lot of old shirts when the Budgie's at large, but a housetrained bird is certainly a nice thing to have. To work this trick, you must think of a word that will never, ever come up in conversation for the command to

defecate. (Actually, "defecate" itself is fine; at least, it isn't something that *my* friends often discuss!) You must also be observant enough to notice the subtle signs that the Budgie is about to defecate, usually a slight squatting just beforehand. At first, content yourself with giving the command every time you see the Budgie doing its business in cage or playpen so that it will begin to associate the word with the act. Later,

A tame bird loves learning tricks because it can use them to amuse itself as well as to get the attention of its owners.

when you're playing with the Budgie and notice that it's about to relieve itself hastily place it atop its cage and give the command. You'll have to be patient and tolerant of accidents for days or weeks, but eventually you should arrive at a point where you can drop the Budgie off at its

cage, give the word, and have it go. Understand, however, that even a well-trained Budgie isn't built to hold it. To prevent accidents, return it to cage or portable playpen every 20 minutes and give it the command.

Let me assure the anxious that accidents are no real problem unless you make a habit of black tie and evening dress at home. Bird droppings come out of washable clothes without any special effort on your part.

No one objects to practical tricks, but some people may have misconceptions about "fun" tricks. It is not cruel to teach your Budgie tricks. In fact, a tame bird loves learning tricks because it can use them to amuse itself as well as to get the attention of its owners. The proof is the many Budgies who will do their tricks when they're playing alone. Actually, it is a kindness to teach tricks because it prevents the bird from becoming bored and listless. In the wild, the Budgie would spend hours each day foraging for food and avoiding predators. In captivity, it needs another use for its clever brain, and what better than tricks which amuse pet and owner alike? Working together to learn tricks forges a deep tie of affection between bird and human. Despite the hundreds of thousands of Budgies in this country, you will have great difficulty purchasing a tame and talking trick bird. Most people simply won't give them up for any price.

The simplest tricks take advantage of the Budgie's

natural actions and curiosity. As a ground bird, the Budgie uses its beak to pull and pick things up, which is quite different from the large tropical parrots who use their feet as "hands" in a manner that looks almost human. Work with, not against, the Budgie's instincts. If you want it to ring a bell or carry a ball, offer it to the beak rather than the claws. These tricks are so simple the Budgie often teaches itself.

Riding a car or electric railroad is also fun. Place your bird on car or train and watch it go! The first few times, it may flutter off uncertainly. Just put it right back on. After a few sessions, the Budgie won't wait for you to holler, "All aboard." It will hop on the car itself and look expectantly for you to start up the ride. Incidentally, in

Climbing is particularly easy to teach your Budgie because it takes advantage of the avian instinct to move up.

Once your pet Budgie has gained confidence and is walking freely up your "ladder" or shoulder, you can move on to holding and head scratching.

some shops you can buy little cars with perches made especially for Budgie riders.

A third trick based on Budgie instincts is climbing. Like all parrots, Budgies are excellent climbers, and they need to be encouraged to enjoy this activity more in captivity where they can't get enough exercise through flying. Climbing is particularly easy to teach because it takes advantage of the avian instinct to move up. Provide a ladder or rope and see what happens. Some Budgies will climb right up

the first time. Others will need some gentle nudging. Return it to the bottom if it cheats by flying up, and reward it with a special treat and lots of praise when it climbs all the way.

In summary: To get a tame *and* trained Budgie who loves you and loves to ham it up for you, be patient and never punish. Reward success with lavish praise and treats of head-scratching or favorite foods. If you spend many short, five to fifteen minute sessions with the Budgie over the course of a few days, you will teach it far more than the person who spends the same amount of time in an hour or two-hour chunks. Always move slowly, and always talk to your bird. Don't think it doesn't understand, it does. And what it understands is that you care enough to make the effort.

To prevent your Budgie from defecating outside of the cage, return it to the cage or portable playpen every 20 minutes and give it a command.

see the bird building go up. Rats and other rodents will want to steal the bird's food, not caring if they contaminate the grain or frighten a breeding pair. Predators from owls to cats will be interested in dining on the Budgies themselves. Cats and rodents may be trapped or shot, but owls, hawks, and eagles are protected by law. (Besides being threatened, these beneficial birds prevent disease by keeping down the rodent population.) In all cases, your building will need to be modified to keep the Budgies in and the predators out. Because birds present such tempting victims to vandals and thieves, you will also need a security system (including an alarm) sufficient to deter break-ins.

In other words, building an outdoor aviary is a grati-fying but specialized enterprise. Fortunately, in recent years, publishers have produced several good books on the subject. The better advanced Budgie handbooks also contain detailed plans for outdoor breeding aviaries.

COMPANIONS

A flight complete with vegetation and other bird species can be a pleasant haven or a deadly disaster! I'd like to pass on a few tips that others have learned through trial and error so you won't have to repeat the same mistakes with your Budgies.

The first rule concerns size. Many commercial aviaries do well by allowing one adult bird per square foot of floor area, but this is definitely a minimum. Never try to squeeze in "just one more." Budgies are sociable, but even they need room to breathe! Overcrowded flights invite fighting, nest-robbing, and disease. Please be assured that a few lively, playful birds will look far more impressive than many listless ones packed so close together they can do nothing but quarrel.

Since Budgies are gentle, they

Overcrowded flights invite fighting, nest-robbing, and disease. A few lively, playful birds will look far more impressive than many listless ones packed so closely together.

are safe with smaller birds who won't bother them. Of course, these smaller birds should be bold enough to be able to make their own way in a flightful of larger creatures! Give delicate, rare finches their own cage, and let the Budgie share with some sassy Zebra or Society Finches. Although much larger, Cockatiels can also live pleasantly with Budgies as long as there is enough room. Sometimes a Cockatiel and a Budgie will become very good friends, actually playing together and preening one another despite the difference in size. Most other parrots, however, are not safe companions for Budgies. Even if a large parrot is "sweet," it shouldn't be

Always try to pair even pairs of birds together, or all of one sex. Never have too many of one sex otherwise disastrous results could occur.

Since Budgies are gentle, they are safe with smaller birds who won't bother them.

Dominant Budgies will probably insist on a first pick of swings, feeders, and nest boxes.

yew, poison or water hemlock, and lily of the valley. Christmastime is a potentially dangerous time since poinsettia, Christmas cherry, and mistletoe are all hazards.

After your careful selection of plants and pals, you can't sit back and take it easy. You still need to keep an eye on how your birds interact in their home. In any closed, limited environment some birds will dominate others in what is often called "the pecking order." Dominant Budgies and Cockatiels will probably insist on a first pick of

Keep a close eye on how your birds interact in an aviary situation. You may have to remove one or two that begin to "bully" the others around.

housed with the Budgie unless it's really an exceptional bird. Most parrot sweethearts are ragingly jealous of avian rivals for your attention and are quite capable of hurting a Budgie when your back is turned.

What about vegetation? Many plants are poisonous to birds, especially to the small, nibbling Budgie. Poisonous plants include dieffenbachia (dumb cane),

swings, feeder, and nest boxes, but they shouldn't be trying to prevent less aggressive birds from nesting, eating, or playing at all. A Budgie bully is almost always trying to tell you something: "We don't have enough feeders, nest boxes, or swings, so I have to hog them all to feel secure." or "There are too many of us in here. If you don't take some

of us out, I can make more room by preventing this weak bird from eating." Budgies are individuals, and on rare occasions, you may encounter the true Budgie bully who just can't get along in the aviary situation. It's unlikely, however. In the vast majority of cases, these amiable birds will do their part in making an aviary a success if you do yours.

Above: Many plants are poisonous to birds. Christmastime is a potentially dangerous time since poinsettia, Christmas cherry, and mistletoe are all hazards.

Right: Several feeders should be placed about the aviary as well as a few on the floor. Any birds that become hurt or bullied around will always go to the floor to eat.

Left: In the vast majority of cases, Budgies are amiable birds will do their part in making an aviary a success.

BREEDING THE BUDGERIGAR

You're captivated by the wonderful Budgerigar and are busily wondering how you can breed some of these terrific birds for your own. You needn't feel obligated to breed—Budgies are prolific in the wild and marvelously abundant in captivity, so you should undertake the job for the sheer pleasure. Of course, there's a bit of work involved, but as far as I know, nothing worthwhile is achieved without some expenditure of effort. Besides, getting there is truly half the fun. The pleasure of working with these charming birds is far greater than the transitory delight of winning a ribbon. Veteran showpeople can tell you that means a great deal, since the high state-of-the-art of Budgerigar breeding makes winning even a novice ribbon for breeding a fine bird a truly great accomplishment.

Before we get into the how-to's, however, let me issue a warning to people who envision Budgie breeding as a good way to make some fast money: Don't hold your breath. The vast majority, if not all breeders, got into the business for love of the bird. Even the large commercial Budgerigar farms frequently started as a hobby that grew because a family or individual was willing to put years of work into developing fine birds and business contacts. If you love birds but really must show a profit, consider Cockatiels. They are as easy

Breeding Budgerigars should be done for the sheer pleasure of the hobby.

to breed and each youngster can be sold for four to eight times the cost of a Budgie. If you don't much care for birds besides your private pet, there are lots of easier ways to make money that don't involve investing in livestock. Many small hobbyists are happy to accept store credit for supplies in exchange for their extra Budgies, and someone just in search of a moneymaker can't compete with that.

As you learn more about Budgies, you'll start hearing a great deal about "English" Budgies. That's because English breeders have done the most to set the standards for high show-quality stock. Even to the unsophisticated eye, the difference in quality is obvious, English Budgies are much larger, with better color and a definite big-breasted shape conforming to the ideal. If you think you might be interested in breeding for show, you'll want to obtain some "English" stock to improve your blood lines. If you want to breed to stock your own aviary or for sale as pets, you don't have to worry about acquiring the larger Budgies since the small ones are just as intelligent and make equally good pets. The choice is yours. In any case, start with healthy, even-tempered adults who are at least one year old. Budgies reach sexual maturity some months beforehand, but if

If you think you might be interested in breeding for show, you'll want to obtain some English stock to improve your blood lines.

When choosing a group of birds for breeding, start with healthy, even tempered adults who are at least one year old.

you settle them down too early, you will have a host of problems such as eggbinding, refusal to incubate eggs, and abandonment of chicks. Like humans, Budgies should be mentally as well as physically adult before they try to bring youngsters into the world.

Don't try to mate a tame, talking Budgie. Many people think that their pets want mates because they are wooing their owners with typical avian courting behaviors such as offering regurgitated food and mating with a human hand. Actually, these are the very birds you *shouldn't* try to mate because they are too emotionally involved with

you to wish to breed. A new Budgie would be viewed as a rival for your attention, not a potential mate. On the other hand, semitame Budgies who are somewhat used to human handling even if they don't much care for it are great breeders because they are less likely to become upset when their owners open their nest boxes to check on the progress of their eggs and chicks.

PREPARING FOR BREEDING

Although Budgies can breed indoors at any time of the year, certain conditions must be met before they will start. First off, the birds must be in top condition, good eaters who are well fed on a healthy diet. Molting Budgies shouldn't be asked

A Budgie must be in top condition, a good eater and fed on a healthy diet before it will start to breed.

Because they are extremely social birds, a single pair of Budgies rarely breed.

to breed because they need all their protein for replacing their feathers. Wait until the molt is over before encouraging them to breed.

Because they are extremely social birds, a single pair of Budgies rarely breed. Even two or three pairs can take their time about settling down. In general, at least 12 to 18 adult Budgies should be present to stimulate breeding. Fortunately for people who want some control over the color and shape of their offspring, that doesn't mean all 18 birds have to be in the same flight! Each pair can do perfectly well in individual cages as long as they can hear and see other Budgies around them. A beginner shouldn't be too horrified by the prospect of starting out with so many birds. The fact that several pairs have synchronized their nesting can make your work a lot easier since you can foster eggs and young chicks of nonfeeding or nervous parents to working nests where they'll be better cared for.

Any rodent or predator problem must be brought under control before setting up for breeding. Budgies aren't interested in raising catfood, so the presence of threatening mammals may prevent them from nesting.

Finally, Budgies must have a nest box. Since they breed in tree cavities in the wild, they have no real nest-building skills, although the female does some chewing to modify the interior to her liking. Fortunately, since they're used to nesting in "found" objects, they settle down nicely in artificial nest boxes. You can buy Budgie nest boxes at pet stores, or you can build your own. A simple plywood box some 10" tall by 6" wide and 6" long, with a 2" diameter hole near the top, works fine. Have a short perch underneath the opening to give feeding birds a place to stand, and chisel a concavity into the floor to prevent the eggs from rolling around. Nest boxes should always be hung high in the cage or flight; otherwise, the Budgies may not accept them.

If your Budgies are al-

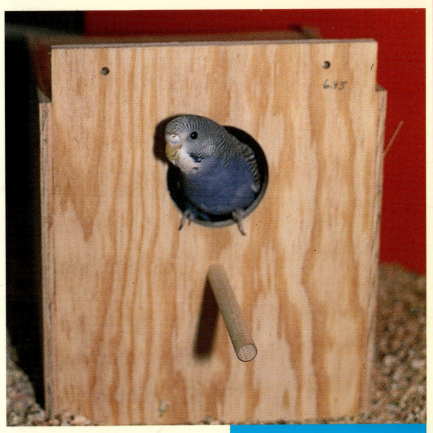

Since Budgies breed in tree cavities in the wild, they have no real nest building skills and must therefore have a next box supplied for them.

ready paired in breeding cages or flying free in a breeding flight, don't give them nest boxes until the other breeding conditions are met. These eager-to-please birds could exhaust themselves, risking infection and death, if they start too early. If your hens and cocks are separated, you may go ahead and put the boxes in with the hens so that they can investigate the nest and maybe indulge in a little chewing to "customize" their homes. Give your hens a couple of weeks to settle into their new cages before adding the cocks. Some people like to introduce the male to the female by placing him in a separate cage where she can look him over for a few days. Divided

breeder cages are available for this purpose; when you see the Budgies flirting through the bars of the divider, you can safely remove it to let them mate.

Occasionally, a hen in a cage won't like the cock you have chosen for her and will attack him. Since she can trap and kill a male she doesn't like, remove him at once. In a flight containing many Budgies, the birds can find their own mates as long as you are careful to put in equal numbers of males and

A pair of breeding Budgies' nest box can be checked for eggs or chicks as long as you are careful.

females. Remember to have twice as many nest boxes as pairs to prevent quarreling.

At the same time that you're introducing pairs, you should be gradually increasing the amount of lighting and protein in the diet. Breeding Budgies should have 14 hours of light a day and a constant supply of fresh soft food and greens. The mineral block should be fresh and clean; replace it immediately when it's consumed.

INCUBATING THE EGGS

When the hen is ready to start laying, she'll spend a great deal of time inside the nest box. If your female Budgie has "disappeared" for several days, you can start making daily checks for eggs. Once laying begins, she will usually lay an egg every other day until she has a complete clutch of four to six eggs.

Sometimes the hen lays extra eggs; clutches of nine and even ten eggs have been recorded. Since it's too exhausting for her to attempt to rear so many chicks at once, you will need to do something about the excess. To find out if you really have a problem, you need to know how many of the eggs are actually fertile. A simple device called a candler is used to test for fertility. More elegant candlers are available from commercial sources, but a home candler is just a box with a bright light bulb inside and a small hole on top. You must wait until ten days after incubation (not laying) to use the candler. Place the egg you want to test in the hole and look through it to the light behind. If you can see reddish "spiders" (blood vessels), you can be sure the egg is fertile. If it's completely clear, it's infertile and should be discarded. It is entirely normal to find an infertile egg or two in a clutch, but you should suspect a nutritional or other problem if *all* of the eggs are infertile.

If you find that you have a hen that has too many fertile eggs, you can transfer some of the eggs into the nests of hens who didn't lay as many. (Mark the transferred eggs with an indelible, odorless pen if you want to keep a record of where they came from!) If you still have leftovers, cull the eggs of inferior birds and keep the eggs of superior specimens. It doesn't matter if a small, unbeautiful hen ends up raising a nest full of a show couple's chicks. She won't know the difference, and you'll be improving the quality of your stock without exhausting the best birds.

Since the hen incubates her eggs day and night, the cock must bring her food. The male Budgie is in most cases an exceptionally solicitous bird, occasionally so concerned with feeding his mate that he neglects to feed himself. Therefore, you

A first hatching, a baby Budgie won't be strong enough to do more than lay around and beg for food from its mother.

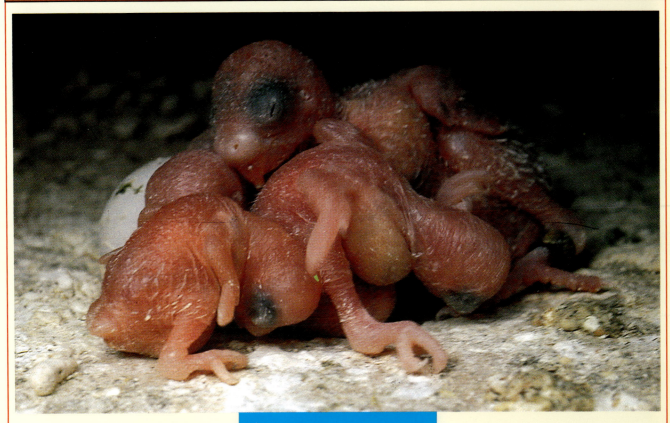

need to check on the cock as well as the eggs when you inspect the cage each day. If he loses too much weight, he may start hiding in the nest box for warmth—where he may remain until he starves to death. Watch out. If a male seems cold or suspiciously underweight, remove him to a hospital cage where he will have a chance to recover. If the hen is nearly ready to hatch her eggs, she can probably take care of them herself. If incubation has just begun, however, you should remove the eggs to prevent her from joining her mate in a fit of exhaustion.

WHEN THE PARENTS RAISE THE YOUNG

The first egg will hatch about 18 days after the hen

Only the mother Budgie feeds newly hatched chicks. When they begin to feather out, the cock will also begin feeding.

starts incubation. You may be able to hear the chick peeping from within its cracked shell and decide to help it out, especially since it seems to be taking an ungodly amount of time to break out. Please resist the temptation! If you have never seen an egg hatch anywhere except on a time-elapsed film on TV, you will probably be surprised to learn that it normally takes a very long time for the tiny chick to emerge; in the case of the Budgie, hatching takes around 36 hours. If you "help" it out too soon,

it won't finish absorbing its nutrient-rich yolk and will therefore be too weak to survive for more than a few hours.

Continue checking the nest box daily, but don't hover over the new chicks or you may make the hen too nervous to care for them. You aren't missing much. Baby Budgies are naked, blind, and downright ugly! At first they won't be strong enough to do more than lay around and beg for food from their mother, who will start them out on her own crop milk. As the chicks grow and feather out, the cock will also begin feeding. If all goes well, their little crops will be plump and full at all times, and their bodies will seem to grow almost in front of your eyes.

If Budgie chicks are not given permanent closed bands before ten days of age (preferably at around five days), their feet will already be too large to allow the band to pass over their toes onto their legs. If you are planning on showing your birds, you should obtain in advance specially coded rings from the American Budgerigar Society to prove that you bred them yourself. Banding isn't hard. Gently holding the chick, first slip the ring over the three long toes, then on back over the short toe onto the lower leg. If the last toe doesn't want to pop free, you may help slip it out with a burnt matchstick.

Soon after ringing day, the young Budgies will start feathering out at an amazing rate. By the end of the fourth week or the beginning of the fifth week, fully feath-

ered chicks should be beginning to leave the nest, although they will still cry to be fed by their parents. If the hen is impatient to lay another clutch, she may become irritable with these ungainly adolescents and try to peck them or pull their feathers to line her nest. In that case, remove them to a separate cage along with the cock so that he can finish raising them. (You can transfer him back to the hen's cage for an hour or two each afternoon for mating.) Of course if all is going well, you can let both parents wean the chicks.

Once they are cracking seed reliably, which should occur around the end of the sixth week, you should remove them to their own cage for sale, pet taming, or whatever. Remember that their instinct is to feed from the ground, so always have plenty of good seed on the floor until they are eating regularly from the feeder.

Your adult birds will live longer and healthier lives if you do not ask them to raise more than two broods a year. When the second brood is finished, you should remove the nest box to prevent the hen from starting the cycle all over again.

FOSTERING AND HANDREARING CHICKS

You don't have to handfeed Budgies to make them into

If all goes well with your Budgie chicks, their little crops will be plump and full at all times, and their bodies will seem to grow almost in front of your eyes.

good pets since they can still become attached to humans if tamed before the tenth or twelfth week of life. Therefore, don't remove chicks from the nest unless you have to. The parents have more time to fuss over their babies than you do! If a young chick falls from its nest, you should warm it in your hands and return it. (It isn't true that human scent causes birds to reject their broods; most birds have relatively poor senses of smell, anyway.) If you aren't sure which nest it came from, just return it to one with babies about the right size. The parents will feed it along with the rest even if you guessed wrong. If it falls out again, you can assume it's being intentionally

If Budgie chicks are not given permanent closed bands before ten days of age, their feet will already be too large to allow the band to pass over their toes onto their legs.

COPING WITH INJURIES AND ILLNESSES

Contrary to what you may have heard, you don't have to give up on a sick Budgie. As more people are developing an interest in pet birds, more vets are studying their problems and diseases. More and more pet Budgies *can* be helped, even cured of such serious illnesses as ornithosis, the so-called "parrot fever." Your chances are better, of course, if you have located an avian vet before an emergency strikes. If you can't get a local recommendation from a bird-keeping friend or club, you can write to the Association of Avian Veterinarians, P.O. Box 299, East Northport, NY 11737, for the name of vets near you who are interested in helping birds. Although the vet trip may cost more than the Budgie, it's often useful to take a new bird in to the vet for a checkup so that the doctor can become familiar with your bird and advise you concerning any potential health problems. If you don't have the Budgie cleared by a vet, it's important to keep it away from any other birds you may own for a full 30 days to make sure it hasn't brought home anything contagious.

Once the Budgie is settled in, the key to avoiding future problems is prevention. Clipped wings, good grooming of beak and claws, and attention to the condition of its environment can prevent injury. An excellent diet and clean home, combined with frequent rests from breeding, help the Budgie resist disease. Boredom, poor diet, or filth encourage disease. Notice the psychological factor. A Budgie should have something to do and someone to do it with; its companion can be a mate with which it rears young, or an avian pal with which it explores the latest toys, or a human friend who teaches it tricks and games, but it must have a companion!

Still, even if we do everything perfectly, sickness and injury can strike, so you need to be aware of the possibility and alert to subtle changes in your Budgie's appearance and personality. A small bird has little room

This photo shows a budgie with a nasal granuloma (growth composed of granulation material) removed.

to store reserves, so it can exhaust itself quickly in the fight against disease. Fast action is often required to save its life. Yet, like most wild animals, Budgies have the infuriating habit of trying to conceal the fact that they don't feel well, a holdover from the wild where predators are quick to take advantage of sick or crippled animals. Often, the first sign that a Budgie is feeling ill is a sudden desire to withdraw from its normal activities. If a pet that's usually playful wants to nap all the time, you need to figure out what's wrong as soon as possible.

Check closely for signs of injury or disease, not that you should attempt to make a diagnosis on your own. Even a vet must often employ lab tests or specialized equipment to pin down the specific cause of a Budgie's problem. For instance, respiratory ailments from mild "colds" to ornithosis can all look much alike; it takes a lab test to determine what disease agent is present and how it should be combatted. As a general rule, you can treat what looks like a relatively mild problem at home by employing the use of isolation and warmth to let the Budgie's body fight the disease itself, while severe symptoms or problems that continue past a day or two call for a trip to the veterinarian's.

Isolation and warmth are best provided by a hospital cage. Nice models are available from advertisers in the bird-fancy magazines and some bird specialty shops, but you can make your own with a small travel cage and heating pad. The typical hospital cage is short, to force the bird to rest, but it's somewhat elongated so that you can put the source of 85 or 90°F heat on one side so that the Budgie can move away if it feels too warm. Often, however, it will be more than glad to recover near the heat in order to reserve its body's fuel supplies, particularly if it's eating poorly. (The normal body temperature of a bird is well over 100°F, so a Budgie with a slight fever can burn through an enormous amount of body fat in days or hours.) Food and water should be in easily accessible spots on the floor, with favorite treats among them to tempt weak appetites. Partially cover the cage to give privacy, a primal need with a sick bird, but leave an opening for fresh air. If you try to give one of the pet store remedies that are added to water, sweeten it with a little orange juice to make it more palatable, or the Budgie may stop drinking. And a time of sickness is no time for a Budgie to give up drinking! Again, if there is no improvement within a couple of days, see your vet for help.

COMMON BUDGIE PROBLEMS

You should be aware of the most common Budgie problems so that you can

Feather picking usually develops in a bird due to dry skin conditions or a dietary condition. However, after the cause has been found and remedied, the feather picking has become a habit that is very hard to break.

take action against them. It is a fact that many Budgies with unclipped wings are injured each year when they fly into walls or other surfaces at full speed. Untame birds are at highest risk, but even a normally calm pet can become startled and forget where it is. Concussion, broken wings, or broken legs are all treatable if you apply first aid for shock and get the bird to a vet as quickly

as possible. The best "shock treatment" is, of course, warmth combined with an enclosed space such as a travel cage to prevent the Budgie from thrashing around and injuring itself further. Cover the cage while it's in transit, for privacy and warmth. Another common injury occurs when ringed or long-nailed Budgies get a foot trapped in a loose hardware staple or other small trap. Quickly staunch blood with direct pressure, extricate the foot if you can, apply first aid for shock, and rush to the vet. Call the office for advice if you can't work the foot free. Try to stay calm. Your Budgie isn't doomed. These birds can live perfectly happy lives with only one foot, although they can no longer position for proper mating and thus cannot breed. A Budgie who has scalded itself by trying to land in boiling water or bathe under a hot tap should also be treated for shock and taken to the vet. A little burn ointment may help soothe it while in transit.

There are several common diseases that you should be on guard against. A particularly pesky one is "French Molt," in which young birds (usually about five to six weeks old) begin an excessive molt of tail and wing feathers. The cause isn't known, although it may be a virus. French Molt is also linked to receiving a low protein crop milk in the early

A particularly pesky disease is French Molt. It is when young birds (usually about five to six weeks old) begin an excessive molt of tail and wing feathers.

weeks of life, so perhaps the viral agent cannot get a foothold in the system if the parents are well fed. It also occurs more often in the offspring of a pair going to nest for the third time without a rest break, which we know exhausts the parents' nutrient reserves and may affect the quality of crop milk they can offer their babies. Good diet and rest periods are therefore the best preventions. Consult your vet for recommendations if the problem has already appeared. Sometimes French Molt clears up by itself after the next molt, but you can't count on it.

At the other end of the spectrum, we have the diseases of old age. The most common are similar to diseases found in older humans: tumors, diabetes, and gout. Since Budgies are extremely susceptible to tumors, you should make a habit of checking your pet for any suspicious lumps and bumps; most are benign and can often be removed. Diabetes, often accompanied by unusual thirst, can often be treated with insulin. Don't be squeamish about learning to inject your pet if that is what's called for; it can lead a happy, normal life with the disease under control. Gout due to kidney or liver dysfunction can cut off the blood supply to its feet, making perching uncomfortable or impossible; unfortunately, we don't know how to prevent or cure this disease, although vet treatment can ease the symptoms. You cannot catch any of these serious diseases from your bird, nor can you give tumors, diabetes, or gout to your pet.

All ages may be bothered by infections and parasites, although quarantining new birds away from any others for 30 days and providing excellent care will prevent many problems. Scaly mite, a microscopic parasite that encrusts the beak or leg with a white deposit, is very common in Budgies. It usually has to be transmitted by direct contact since it spends its whole life on the bird, so isolating the affected Budgies will prevent the disease from spreading. If treating the affected area with a small amount of mineral oil doesn't cure the problem, a prescription medication from the vet should finish the job. Red mites, which feed on birds at night and then leave to conceal themselves in the cracks of the cage and nest boxes during the day, can cause itching and discomfort in older birds while stealing so much blood from nestlings that the vulnerable babies die. If you suspect red mites, cover the cage with a

Many Budgies with unclipped wings are injured each year when they fly into walls or other surfaces at full speed.

white cover at night and shine a light on it later; if the mites are present, you'll see tiny red specks moving across the cloth as they leave your Budgies. To rid yourself of these pesky critters, you must clean all cracks and crevices of perches, nest boxes, swings, feeders, toys, and cages. A real pain! It's better to prevent an infestation in the first place by buying one of the many fine sprays or "bird protector" devices sold in pet stores.

A third common parasite, *Giardia*, makes its home in a Budgie's intestines, often causing poor digestion or large, discolored, smelly feces. After examining the wastes to diagnose the problem, the vet can prescribe a medication to kill the parasite.

Finally, we come to the respiratory diseases. You cannot hope to do much more on your own than try to make a rough determination of the severity of the problem. If the Budgie is a little sleepy and sneezy, putting it in the hospital cage for a day or two may be all you need. But if it has a nasal discharge, or its symptoms have persisted despite warmth and isolation, you must go to a vet who can make tests in order to prescribe the proper drug.

One possible respiratory infection is properly called Ornithosis, or Clamydiosis, although it is known to the public as Psittacosis, or "Parrot Fever." Any bird can carry it, not just parrots, so the name is unfair

and inaccurate. (Pigeons, both feral and domesticated, seem to be the number-one carriers of the disease.) A diagnosis of ornithosis is no longer a cause for panic, since the Budgie will usually recover quickly when treated with modern drugs. In the unlikely event that you contract the disease from your Budgie, today's medication will cure you as well. Of course, if you contract flu or pneumonia-like symptoms, you have to do your part and let your doctor know that you keep birds so that he or she can test for the possibility.

With care, quick thinking, and a little luck, your pet Budgie can be one of the growing number of feathered senior citizens.

Although disease and injury will always be with us, I hope you have been encouraged by our quick look at some of the advances in avian medical science. A sick bird doesn't have to be a dead bird, not if you keep a cool head and seek timely help. With care, quick thinking, and a little luck, your pet Budgie can be one of the growing number of feathered senior citizens.